Beneath the Surface

EMBRACE THE LAYERS OF YOUR INNER BEAUTY

TEJUMADE A. D. OGUNMOKUN

EDITED BY
NICOLE QUEEN

VISION PUBLISHING
HOUSE

"He has made everything beautiful in its time."

ECCLESIASTES 3:11 KJV

Contents

Introduction

Hey there, beautiful woman!

I'm so honored that you took the time to pick up this book. Your journey towards embracing your inner beauty starts right here, and I couldn't be more excited to be a part of it.

This book, "Beneath the Surface: Embrace the Layers of Your Inner Beauty," is more than just a guide; it's a companion on your journey to recognizing and celebrating your inner beauty. While makeup and external appearances can be a source of joy and self-expression, it's crucial to remember that true beauty radiates from within. This book aims to help you see that your inner beauty is just as important, if not more.

According to Dove, one in three women feel pressured to alter their appearance because of what they see online, even when they know the images are fake or AI-generated. The rise of AI poses one of the greatest threats to real beauty in the last 20 years, meaning authentic representation is more important than ever. We live in a world where the digital portrayal of beauty often overshadows the real, and this book is here to remind you that your natural beauty, both inside and out, is invaluable.

This book is for all the strong, hardworking women across the globe. Whether you're a busy professional, a dedicated mother, a student, or someone finding their way in this world, this book is for you. There is no requirement for the woman who reads this book. It's for anyone looking to feel loved, embraced, and supported while going through their inner transformation journey.

In the pages that follow, you'll discover many different journeys beneath the surface. Each chapter is designed to guide you through various aspects of embracing your inner beauty. We'll explore stories from women just like you, delve into practical tips, and provide you with the inspiration needed to truly love and accept yourself from the inside out.

As you begin this journey, remember that you are beautiful just as you are. Embrace every layer of your inner beauty, and let this book be your guide and friend along the way. Together, we'll uncover the beauty that lies beneath the surface, and you'll see that you are truly radiant in every possible way.

Beauty Beyond Appearance

I n today's world, many people, young and old, are influenced by what they see on TV and in magazines. The major influences on beauty standards often come from global trends and celebrities. It's essential to be confident in ourselves and not let popular trends interfere with our unique concepts of beauty.

For example, Brazilian Butt Lifts (BBLs) are very popular in this day and time. Everywhere you go, you may see women who have undergone this surgery to enhance their looks. However, some women don't do their research before getting the surgery and may experience significant pain afterward. This pain can be temporary for some, while for others, it might last a lifetime. We must ask ourselves if it is truly worth it. Our purpose on Earth should not be defined by our exterior appearance but by who we are as individuals. Let's break free from narrow beauty standards by embracing self-reflection and empathy towards others.

EMBRACING DIVERSITY

True beauty is not limited to size, shape, or color but resides in the hearts of those who dare to be unique and embrace their individuality. To my brown-skinned ladies, let's celebrate the different shades of black. You are strong and amazing from the lightest shade to the darkest. If you didn't know, let me tell you why. My beautiful albino sisters, your rare genetic beauty radiates from within. Your lower pigmentation results in a pale or white appearance, enhancing your striking features. Your eyes, shining bright with hues of blue, hazel, or even pink, sparkle like diamonds. To those with caramel complexions, your skin glows with a warm sun-kissed radiance, like the soft shimmer of gold in the sunlight. For those with mahogany skin, you radiate an aura of sophistication and poise with your luxurious deep brown, accented by warm undertones of red and gold, evoking a sense of regal refinement. Chestnut brown beauties, your skin is flawless, and your features are unique. You have a natural glow that can't be replicated, and your smile can light up any room. Your presence is undeniable.

Often, people's perception of beauty is defined solely by one's physical appearance, but this narrow definition overlooks the true essence of beauty, which lies in one's character and personality. How we treat others is a true reflection of our beauty. Our self-perception and emotions towards ourselves significantly impact our journey towards personal growth, affecting how we approach challenges, make decisions, and navigate life's obstacles. By fostering a positive and compassionate relationship with ourselves, we can create an environment conducive to growth and development.

A STORY OF SELF-LOVE

Let's dive into a story about a young woman named Natasha, who is fun, honest, and outgoing:

> "Oh my goodness, this pimple is huge! I can't believe I have a disgusting pimple the day before school begins!" she yelled while sadly looking at herself in the mirror.

> "Girl, what is going on with you?" Natasha's mother yelled from the other room. Natasha slowly walked over to her mom.

"Do you see this giant thing on my face? This is unbelievable. I just want to go to my room and cry."

Ms. Tina hugged her daughter, holding her chin up and looking her directly in the eyes.

"Girl, you are beautiful with or without this pimple, which will eventually go away. This pimple on your face does not determine who you are. It may be big to you, but I guarantee you that no one other than yourself will notice it."

"You are right, Mom. Thank you so much for always being there to encourage me!" Natasha said.
She washed her face and got her new clothes ready for school.

"Goodnight, Mom," she said, walking over to give her a kiss on the cheek.

"Goodnight," Ms. Tina replied.

Natasha went to school the next day, and all her friends were happy to see her. She even made new friends through her bright, outgoing personality. After school, she ran into the house with great excitement and told Ms. Tina how amazing her day was.

"You were right, Mom," Natasha said. "No one even noticed my pimple. Can you believe it?"

"Girl, I told you no one would notice," Ms. Tina replied. "I'm so glad you didn't let that determine the outcome of your day."

Natasha's story highlights the significance of self-love and the influence of our actions on others. It demonstrates that a positive attitude and a strong support system can lead to a more fulfilling life.

May you embrace who you are, love yourself unconditionally, and remember that true beauty lies beyond the surface.

"

Outer beauty attracts, but inner beauty captivates.

- Kate Angell

"

Nurturing Your Inner Glow

Inner beauty flourishes with consistent self-care practices. For myself, daily prayer is a simple yet powerful practice that sets the tone for my day. By starting and ending each day with meaningful prayer, it helps me navigate through life's toughest challenges.

Listening to inspiring messages from Joel Olsteen, Sarah Jakes Roberts, or my pastor Fred Wyatt (depending on the day), energizes my spirit as I prepare to work from home or in the building. Not only does prayer and hearing the word of God uplift my day at work, but it also helps in my personal life and well-being. Reading scriptures like Galatians 6:9, "Let us not become weary in doing good, for at the proper time we will reap the harvest if we do not give up," gives me strength and guidance to continue doing good things while being good to others. As no good deed goes unseen, everything we do in life shapes our future.

It is important to fill my cup with positive influences as this shapes my day and life. I also find value in being surrounded by inspiring, uplifting individuals such as family, friends, or mentors.

By surrounding yourself with positive light and influences, you can only lead to a more positive perspective and outcome. Conversely, if you surround yourself with negativity, your perspective will become negative based on your surroundings and influences. This is why having a strong foundation of positive influences will shape any individual into a better person.

Reflect on your own experiences. Have you ever found yourself in an uncomfortable situation that felt unbearable or overwhelming? How did you navigate through it? Give yourself some time to reflect on what positive factors or influences helped you. If you can identify these factors, I encourage you to rinse and repeat whatever you did to get through that challenging time. Continue to do that when other life challenges arise.

When you persistently apply positive pressure towards cultivating your life challenges by constantly pushing yourself to grow and improve, you'll be able to overcome any obstacle and achieve greatness. Laughter has the power to bring people together while creating a sense of connection and happiness. To have a happier day, try to laugh more by focusing on the positive aspects of life and finding joy in everyday situations.

A STORY OF COMPASSION

Let's look at Tamar's perspective on shaping her day while working at a demanding company, where she sometimes feels overlooked and under-valued, even though she excels at her job.

"Thank you for calling, Tamar speaking. How may I help you?" Tamar answered the phone professionally.

"Yeah. This is Mr. James speaking. This is a sorry darn company! I'm so tired of y'all nonsense. I can't believe this again. I can't even sign into my account, and this is the millionth time I'm calling you darn people. I sure hope you're competent enough to help me because all the others seem like they don't have a clue!" Mr. James yelled with hostility in his voice.

"I'm so sorry you feel that way, Mr. James. However, I'll be more than eager to help you resolve this issue," Tamar responded, taking a deep breath and asking God to guide her during the call.

"Yeah, yeah, yeah. I heard that saying before. All of you say the same darn thing, and nothing ever gets done," Mr. James continued.

Tamar calmly reminded herself to remain positive. She placed herself in his shoes, not knowing his circumstances. For all she knew, Mr. James could have lost a loved one or been going through something major. Despite his tone, she responded with kindness and patience, while thinking of a happy place. Tamar set the tone by filling her mind with thoughts of compassion, love, and laughter.

"By the way, I don't think I had the chance to ask you, but aside from this, may I ask how your day is going?" she asked.

"Wow, well that's a first," Mr. James responded, tearing up. "No one ever asked me that. You're the first person to ask me that question all day."

"I'm so sorry to hear that, Mr. James, but I'm happy that I was the first. Let's try to continue making this day better for you. I'll do whatever I can to help," Tamar said, guiding him through the steps to resolve his issue. "Mr. James, I see that all you need is a link to reset your passcode. I'll send this to you now and stay on the phone to ensure you can reset it. Is that okay?" she asked.

"Yes, that's okay. You know, you are the first to be so patient and kind with me," Mr. James replied.

"Well, that's what I'm here for, Mr. James," Tamar responded.

"Oh my God, this is great. I was able to reset it, and I'm in my account. Thank you! You really made my day," Mr. James exclaimed.

Knowing she turned a negative into a positive, Tamar felt joy and laughter in her heart.

"It was my pleasure, Mr. James," she said.

Later that week, Tamar received an exceptional survey, which led to additional positive feedback within her position.

When you choose to respond with empathy and laughter during a difficult situation, you have the power to change the outcome into an uplifting experience that exhibits your remarkable character.

SELF-AWARENESS AND A POSITIVE MINDSET

Self-awareness is not only about recognizing your strengths and weaknesses but also understanding how others perceive you. This includes being aware of your body language, tone of voice, and the way you communicate with others. By developing this ability, you can shape the relationships you have and build stronger connections with the people around you.

Let's consider, Tiffany, for example:

Tiffany is originally from Queens, New York, and is very vibrant. She talks fast and, unknowingly, speaks with an assertive tone due to her upbringing. Recently, she moved to Mississippi for school, where others see her as rude and sometimes obnoxious because they are not used to her fast-paced and raw communication style.

Adjusting to her new environment, Tiffany realized she needed to adapt to fit in better with her surroundings. As a result, Tiffany began to study her environment more closely and worked on not sounding so aggressive, understanding that her fast-talking demeanor might be overwhelming for her new, slower-paced community. This process allowed Tiffany to learn and grow in her new environment; also, others around her learned and grew from her.

The ability to learn and grow from people of different backgrounds and walks of life creates a lasting and meaningful impact on cultural diversity. We will often face challenges similar to what Tiffany experienced when we travel or encounter different faces, places, cultures, or ways of thinking. Each country, state, and area has its unique way of life, which is why it's essential to embrace differences and be accepting of others. By accepting differences in others, we show that we are eager and willing to love and learn from one another without passing judgment. The ability to remain positive while growing through changes in environments will set the tone for embracing diverse backgrounds.

ACCOUNTABILITY AND EMPOWERMENT

Embracing accountability means taking responsibility for your actions and their outcomes while learning and growing from them. It is not about blaming, shaming, or gaslighting others into believing they are the cause of the problem. Instead, it's about taking ownership of what happens because of your choices in life, which ultimately affects others.

Let's consider, Mariah, for example:

Mariah has a natural talent for nurturing and supporting others. Most see her as a mother figure, even though she isn't a mother herself. She serves as a counselor to most of her friends and is the go-to person for advice. She shares her expertise willingly because it's a gift she truly enjoys.

One day, on her way to work, Mariah encountered an old childhood friend named Destiny. Despite Destiny wearing large glasses and trying to hide her face, Mariah noticed her tense body language and tone of voice as she spoke on the phone at the bus stop.

"Destiny, is that you?" Mariah asked as she walked up to her. Destiny looked down, attempting to hide her face, and responded hesitantly, "Yes."

Mariah, noticing a bruise through Destiny's glasses, asked, "Is everything okay?"

Destiny, still on the phone, abruptly replied to the person she was speaking to, "I have to go."

Mariah, speaking with confidence and guidance, said, "You know you can talk to me about anything, right?"

Destiny began to cry, moved by the concern from her old friend. "I just don't know what to do. I don't know where to go," she said, shouting. "He keeps putting his hands on me, and I have no family and nowhere to run. I'm so embarrassed you had to see me like this," Destiny added, tears streaming down her face.

Mariah hugged her friend and referred her to a nearby women's shelter. She called off work and drove Destiny to the shelter, which was able to accept her immediately. While Destiny processed her paperwork, Mariah gave her a business card and $300 in cash.

"Call me anytime if you need me. Just know that you are beautiful and you are loved. I love you," Mariah said before leaving.

A few months later, Mariah received a call from Destiny.

"Hello," Mariah answered. "Hi, this is Destiny. I just want you to know that your act of kindness put me in a better state. I now work at the shelter you sent me to. Can you believe it? They have a transition program that helps you find work and a place to stay. Next week, I'll be moving into my new apartment. I just wanted to say thank you so much for telling me I am loved and for being a friend."

Destiny continued, "Even though we hadn't talked or seen each other in years, I'm in a much better place because of your act of kindness. You didn't judge me for my struggle, but uplifted me. Thank you so much, Mariah. I really appreciate you. You didn't have to do that, but you did."

"You're welcome, girl. This literally made my day. I was wondering when you were going to call me, but something kept telling me you were okay. Thank you for confirming everything I believed and prayed for in advance for you," Mariah replied.

Through Mariah's act of kindness, she experienced a sense of purpose and understanding, demonstrating the significance of using our abilities for good. Her example inspires us to adopt a similar mindset, fostering a spirit of compassion by enhancing the well-being of those we touch.

May you be inspired to let your light shine brightly enough to uplift another person in their time of need.

Embracing Imperfections

W hen thinking of your scars, remember that they tell a story. Nobody knows what you have been through. Nobody knows where the scar on your stomach or the scar on your face came from. Or, what about the dark circles under your eyes? They could be from a lack of sleep, being a new mom, or even hereditary factors.

Everyone has scars, and that's what makes us unique.

Consider a person with a speech impediment who may speak differently. Don't judge them for how they talk. They might know a lot—perhaps more than you could imagine! They could be an expert, genius, or even a lawyer. Their flaw, something they were born with and cannot control, should not define who they are. Instead, allow their character and how they treat others to define them as a person.

We have to, as human beings, learn to embrace what makes us different. When you accept yourself for whatever it is that you bring, that allows you to stand out. Your imperfections make you unique. In today's world, don't let your imperfections make you insecure. Instead, enhance those traits and allow them to grow and stand out, making you the best version of yourself.

We must learn to embrace what makes us different. When you accept yourself for whatever it is that you bring, that allows you to stand out. Your imperfections make you unique. In today's world, don't let your imperfections make you insecure. Instead, enhance those traits and allow them to grow and stand out, making you the best version of yourself.

EXTERNAL PRESSURES TO CONFORM

There are many pressures in today's time to look a certain way. Years ago, there was pressure for everyone to be skinny, to look like the girls on magazine covers. But now, different shapes and sizes are being accepted.

Today's trend in 2024 is focused on appreciating everyday body types. You don't have to look like a model all the time. You don't have to be perfect. It's okay to just be yourself. When you can be yourself without worrying about how you look, it allows people to feel connected to you. It's in those transparent moments that people feel comfortable enough to let loose and relax, knowing that everything isn't perfect.

The way we should respond to external pressures in today's world is by not striving for perfection. In this world, nothing is perfect. Not even the roads we walk on are perfect. The only thing perfect is the way God created life, and He accepts us for our imperfect moments and sins. He knows that we are all unique and not perfect. We have to respond to pressures by being our unique, authentic selves. Trying to fit into everyday pressures will drive you crazy. It's too much to keep up with.

Stop trying to fit into everyday pressures. It is not necessary. Just be you. Be the true, authentic, 'happy' you. That is what makes you unique. Whatever makes you happy, whatever makes you smile, whatever lights your day, that is what matters.

We don't have to be what society wants us to be because society changes every day. Every day there are new trends, new data, and new techniques. It's impossible to adapt to everyday changes. Just do what works best for you while letting your light shine bright!

SELF-CONFIDENCE AND SELF-ACCEPTANCE

To overcome insecurities and find strategies for confidence and self-acceptance, you must dive into your true self. Look at yourself in the mirror every day and affirm:

 I am *beautiful*. I am *amazing*. I am *smart*. I am *loved*. I am *fearfully and wonderfully made*. I am *the best* at what I do. I am *perfect* the way God created me. I can do all things through Christ! No weapon formed against me shall prosper. Everything I touch prospers. I will prosper in everything I do. I decree and declare greatness over my life.

Say these things to yourself every single day. Accept yourself for who you are. When you do this, you build self-confidence. If you wake up thinking negative thoughts, that's the mindset you will reciprocate. But when you speak positive affirmations, it changes and shapes your day and outcome in life.

Self-love starts with you. To love others and for others to love you back, you must first love yourself. Say positive affirmations, stay positive throughout the day, and bask in that positive environment. Life will place many obstacles along your path, but with a strong belief system, confidence, and inner strength, you can overcome them. Learn to love yourself, speak positive affirmations, and be kind to yourself and others. Each morning when you wake up, remind yourself of these things.

Accepting yourself for who you are is crucial for building self-confidence. When you genuinely look at yourself and speak these affirmations, you start to believe them, and this belief radiates outwardly, affecting how others perceive you. When you embrace your imperfections and see them as unique traits, it fosters a sense of acceptance and love within you. Others will see this love and confidence, and it will attract positive interactions.

The journey of self-acceptance requires constant reinforcement. Say to yourself, "I am different. I am beautiful. I am amazing. I am a child of God." Own your identity. This practice changes your day and shapes your mindset. When you accept yourself, others will naturally gravitate towards your authenticity and positivity.

In overcoming insecurities, remember that self-love starts with you. Treat yourself kindly and be gentle with your imperfections. Positive self-talk, prayers, and affirmations help maintain a positive outlook. They serve as a buffer against the challenges and obstacles life throws at you. Speaking kindly to yourself helps cultivate inner strength, enabling you to face daily tests with resilience.

The more you embrace yourself, the more you can accept others. This acceptance fosters a more inclusive and compassionate environment. Treating yourself with love and respect sets a standard for how you treat others. As you grow in self-acceptance, your ability to appreciate and accept the differences in others also grows.

SEEKING PROFESSIONAL HELP

Sometimes, life can be overwhelming. You might go through family deaths, become a first-time mom, or face significant changes that disrupt your daily routine. Talking to someone can help. Whether it's a counselor, a trusted friend, or journaling, expressing your feelings is crucial.

In the African-American community, there has been a stigma around seeking help, but it's important to overcome that. Do whatever you need to continuously grow and prosper in life.

If you ever feel overwhelmed, consult with someone positive in your life. It could be a pastor, a close friend, a family member, or anyone you trust. Letting out your feelings helps you heal and overcome insecurities. Seeking professional assistance when needed is vital. Do what works for you, and remember, nobody can tell you what to do, but getting help when life is challenging is essential.

Embrace your imperfections, love yourself, and let your light shine brightly. You are unique, and that's what makes you beautiful.

"

Beauty is not in the face;
beauty is a light in the heart.

- Kahlil Gibran

"

Authentic Beauty in a Filtered World

In today's digital age, the lines between social media and reality have become increasingly blurred. As we scroll through our feeds, we are bombarded with images of seemingly perfect lives and flawless appearances. It's easy to forget that these images are often curated and edited to present the best possible version of oneself. Therefore, it's important to understand the contrast between the filtered world of social media and the authenticity of real life, emphasizing the importance of understanding this distinction for our self-image and well-being.

SOCIAL MEDIA VS. REALITY

When defining and exploring the difference between social media and reality, consider a picture on social media that is edited with filters or Photoshop. As a model, I know firsthand that photographers often stamp pictures as "raw and unedited" to signify their authenticity. They want you to know that the image is untouched and represents their work accurately. Many photographers do not want their unedited photos posted because it reflects their professional standards.

When you're on social media, understand that what you see is often not the raw, unedited version of a person. Some pictures are edited to remove imperfections. I've personally seen my imperfections smoothed over in photos. Photographers prefer not to post unedited work to maintain their professional image. This should remind us that social media does not always reflect reality. Someone might have scars or cellulite that are hidden in photos, or their skin might be edited to look flawless. It's important to recognize the difference between social media and reality.

We all have lives outside of social media. Social media is an online presence, not reality. Don't take it too seriously. Life existed before social media, and back then, we valued what people said about someone in the community and how they treated others. Social media can make it seem like everything is online, but we must remember the importance of real-life interactions and relationships.

In the past, everyone aspired to look like the skinny models on magazine covers. Today, beauty standards have shifted, and we see more acceptance of different body types. Curvier bodies are now celebrated, and that's a wonderful thing! However, the pressure to conform to beauty standards still exists, with many young women feeling the need to alter their bodies through cosmetic surgery to fit in.

To young girls growing up in this era, I say:

 Love yourself first. Embrace who you are. Your beauty is not defined by the size of your behind or your chest. It's not about being skinny or curvy.

Your beauty is defined by who you are as a person, how you treat others, your perseverance, and your determination. How you treat your parents and your kindness towards others define your beauty more than your physical appearance.

Your inner self is what makes you truly beautiful. While society might highlight external features, what truly matters is how you treat others and how you see yourself. Your exterior is just a small part of who you are.

Remember, the way you interact with others and your inner character are the true measures of beauty.

To the young girls who might look up to women with surgically enhanced bodies, I say this to you:

 Know that you don't need to alter yourself to be beautiful. Focus on your inner qualities and how you treat others. That's what makes you stand out.

Your inner beauty is far more significant than your outer appearance. Embrace who you are and let your true self shine.

AUTHENTIC SELF-EXPRESSION

Authentic self-expression means being able to effortlessly and confidently be who you are without worries, doubts, or shame. It involves sharing your stories with others, even if they are not the most glamorous or highlight-worthy. These stories are part of your journey, turning tests into testimonies. When you define your authentic self-expression, it means being transparent in a world that often values perfection.

Transparency allows others to relate to you. Everyone faces challenges and limitations, but acknowledging them and expressing your true self despite these obstacles shows strength and resilience. These challenges are temporary, and overcoming them allows you to flourish like a butterfly. When people see your journey, they can admire your presence, your existence, and your perseverance. They can appreciate that you faced difficulties, overcame them, and chose to share your story, helping others in the process.

Being your authentic self leads to genuine connections. You should always embrace your true self without filters or pretense, regardless of race or culture. Embrace your authentic self because you never know who is watching, looking up to you, or learning from your journey. Someone out there is observing your story, seeing you overcome your battles, and becoming the best version of yourself.

———

Be you. Be your authentic self and don't look back. Someone out there is inspired by you. Your story can touch lives and create change simply because you chose to be genuine and true to yourself.

> **"**
>
> *Whole life is a search for beauty. But, when the beauty is found inside, the search ends and a beautiful journey begins.*
>
> *- Harshit Walia*
>
> **"**

Cultivating Inner Strength

W hen exploring strategies for developing inner strength and resilience amidst challenges, it's essential to recognize that everyone will face obstacles at some point. Regardless of who you are, where you come from, or your age, you will encounter hurdles that require you to learn how to overcome them. These challenges might cause you to detour or reroute, but reaching a detour doesn't mean the journey is over. It means you must get up, think of a new plan, figure it out, and overcome it.

If you are the type of person who doesn't allow anything to get in your way, you will excel in whatever you do. In life, we will face setbacks and obstacles that disrupt our plans. Sometimes, despite our best efforts to plan every detail, life has a different path in store. While planning is crucial for setting a foundation and providing structure, it's equally important to be flexible and adaptable when things don't go as planned.

When you encounter setbacks, it's crucial to focus on what you do next rather than what you didn't do. I encourage you to review your goals, look at your prayer list, reflect on your affirmations, and identify what motivates you. Understanding your purpose—whether it's to serve others, inspire, or support—can help you navigate obstacles. Having a clear goal in mind makes it easier to overcome setbacks, even if it's not always easy. Planning allows you to adapt and continue moving forward despite difficulties.

I've faced several setbacks in life, including financial hurdles that took me by surprise. During those challenging months, I had to take a deep breath, narrow down my focus, and use my financial planner. Limiting expenses and using backup plans taught me the importance of having a savings plan. This experience, though uncomfortable, put me in a better financial position and reinforced the value of preparedness.

Everyone experiences setbacks, but it's how you respond that matters. Embrace a mindset of determination and tunnel vision, focusing on the end goal. You may be in a difficult place now, but with perseverance, you'll reach the end of the tunnel and be able to look back and share your journey with others, helping them navigate similar challenges.

Showing resilience amidst challenges is something all women are capable of. I tip my hat to all women, whether mothers or not, for their strength and determination. Surround yourself with positive, uplifting people who have faced similar challenges. Talking about your experiences is valuable for growth. Keeping everything bottled up will only lead to an explosion. Open up, share your struggles, and you'll find support and solutions.

Remember, at the end of the day, you will get through this. Put on your positive hat and focus on tunnel vision. With this mindset, you will see yourself overcoming obstacles and emerging stronger on the other side.

EMPOWERMENT THROUGH SELF-LOVE

Self-love fosters empowerment and self-fulfillment. Believing in your ability to make choices, overcome obstacles, and create positive change is crucial. When you respect and love yourself, you become more optimistic and outgoing, even in the face of challenges.

Having an optimistic view makes a significant difference. When setbacks occur, avoid creating a pity party for yourself. Instead, maintain a positive attitude. It might be difficult to stay optimistic in the moment, but having faith and a positive mindset will help you get through it. Decree and declare positive outcomes, even in challenging situations. Pray, bind what you don't want, and release what you desire. Claim what is rightfully yours, and trust that God will guide you.

Patience is key during challenging times. Take deep breaths, think about the bigger picture, and remember that your current situation is temporary. With an optimistic outlook, you become unstoppable. Your inner strength and determination will help you overcome anything that comes your way.

Loving yourself is vital for empowerment. When you value yourself, you set higher standards and won't settle for less. Self-love equips you with the strength and resilience to face life's challenges head-on.

THE JOURNEY THROUGH FINANCIAL DIFFICULTIES

I've had my share of financial hurdles. There were times when unexpected expenses left me in a difficult financial situation. These moments were not comfortable at all. I remember questioning God, asking why I was going through such difficulties when I had plans that required financial stability. These experiences taught me the importance of having a financial plan and saving for unexpected events.

During these challenging times, I took a deep breath, reevaluated my finances, and cut down on unnecessary expenses. I leaned on my backup plans, which helped me stay afloat. These experiences taught me the value of having a savings plan and being prepared for unexpected financial setbacks. Though these times were tough, they made me more resilient and better prepared for future challenges.

When facing setbacks, it's essential to adopt a mindset of determination and tunnel vision. Focus on the end goal and push through the obstacles. You might be in a tough spot now, but with persistence, you will reach the end of the tunnel and be able to reflect on your journey. Sharing your experiences with others who are facing similar challenges can provide them with the support and guidance they need.

The company you keep plays a significant role in how you handle life's challenges. Surround yourself with positive, uplifting individuals who can offer support and guidance. Talking about your struggles with someone who has faced similar challenges can provide valuable insights and help you navigate your way through difficult times.

Remember, you are not alone. There is strength in community and in sharing your experiences. By opening up and seeking support, you can find the strength to overcome any obstacle.

Affirmations are powerful tools that can help you maintain a positive outlook, even during tough times. Every morning, look at yourself in the mirror and remind yourself of your worth. Say, "I am beautiful. I am strong. I am capable." These affirmations can help you start your day with a positive mindset and prepare you to face any challenges that come your way.

When you encounter setbacks, remind yourself of your "why" and focus on the positive aspects of your life. This practice can help you stay grounded and motivated, even when things are difficult.

STRATEGIES FOR BUILDING RESILIENCE

Building resilience requires practical strategies that you can implement in your daily life. Here are five tips to help you cultivate inner strength and resilience:

1. Stay Flexible: Life is unpredictable, and things don't always go as planned. Stay flexible and be willing to adapt when necessary.

2. Seek Support: Don't be afraid to ask for help when you need it. Whether it's talking to a friend, family member, or professional, seeking support can provide you with valuable insights and encouragement.

3. Practice Self-Care: Taking care of yourself is crucial for building resilience. Make time for activities that you enjoy and that help you relax and recharge.

4. Stay Positive: Maintaining a positive outlook can help you navigate through tough times. Focus on the good in your life and practice gratitude regularly.

5. Learn from Setbacks: View setbacks as opportunities for growth. Reflect on what you can learn from each experience and how you can apply those lessons in the future.

CELEBRATING SMALL WINS

Recognize and celebrate your small achievements along the way. Each step you take towards your goals is a victory. Celebrating these small wins can boost your confidence and keep you motivated. Acknowledge your progress and give yourself credit for your hard work and perseverance.

Imagine each goal as a mountain. As you climb, there are various milestones. Reaching each milestone, no matter how small, is an accomplishment. Celebrating these moments helps you see how far you've come, providing the encouragement needed to keep pushing forward. Take time to reflect on these victories. Write them down in a journal, share them with a friend, or simply take a moment to appreciate yourself. These small celebrations reinforce your efforts and remind you that you are capable of achieving your larger goals.

In times of struggle, looking back at your small wins can provide a much-needed morale boost. They serve as evidence of your ability to overcome challenges and progress. Use these memories as fuel to push through current and future obstacles. Every small victory is a building block for your confidence, helping you to build a solid foundation of self-belief.

Remember that it's okay to reward yourself for these achievements. Treat yourself to something special, take a break to do something you enjoy, or simply acknowledge your success internally. Rewards can be powerful motivators, and giving yourself something to look forward to can make the journey toward your goals more enjoyable and fulfilling.

FINDING STRENGTH IN FAITH

Faith can be a powerful source of strength during challenging times. Whether it's through prayer, meditation, or spiritual practices, finding solace in your faith can provide comfort and guidance. Trust that God has a plan for you and that you are never alone in your journey. Lean on your faith to find the strength and courage to face any obstacle.

Faith acts as an anchor, grounding you amid life's storms. It provides a sense of purpose and direction when you feel lost or overwhelmed. Engaging in daily spiritual practices such as prayer or meditation can help you center your thoughts, reduce stress, and gain clarity on your path forward. These practices remind you that you are part of something greater than yourself and that a higher power is guiding you.

Consider the story of Job from the Bible. Despite losing everything —his wealth, his family, and his health—Job's faith in God remained unwavering. He endured immense suffering but continued to trust in God's plan. Eventually, Job's faith was rewarded, and he was blessed with even greater prosperity than before. This story teaches us that faith can sustain us through our darkest hours and that perseverance, grounded in faith, can lead to greater rewards.

Personal stories of faith can also be inspiring. Reflect on times when your faith has helped you overcome difficulties. Perhaps there was a moment when a prayer was answered in an unexpected way or a time when meditation brought you peace during a crisis. These experiences reinforce the power of faith in your life.

In addition to personal spiritual practices, connecting with a faith community can provide additional support. Attending church services, joining prayer groups, or participating in spiritual retreats can strengthen your faith and create a network of support. These communities offer a sense of belonging and mutual encouragement, reinforcing your resilience.

Faith also encourages a positive mindset. Believing that you are guided and protected by a higher power can reduce feelings of fear and anxiety. It allows you to face challenges with confidence, knowing that you are never truly alone. This perspective can transform how you approach obstacles, turning potential setbacks into opportunities for growth and learning.

THE ROLE OF COMMUNITY IN BUILDING RESILIENCE

Community support can play a significant role in building resilience. Surround yourself with people who uplift and encourage you. Participate in community activities or groups where you can connect with others who share similar goals and values. Building strong relationships within your community can provide a sense of belonging and support.

A supportive community acts as a safety net, catching you when you fall and helping you bounce back stronger. These relationships provide emotional support, practical assistance, and a sense of shared experience. Whether it's friends, family, colleagues, or members of a social group, having people who understand and care about you can make a significant difference in your ability to cope with stress and adversity.

Engaging with your community can take many forms. Volunteering for local organizations, joining clubs or interest groups, and attending community events are all ways to build connections. These activities not only provide social support but also give you a sense of purpose and contribution. Knowing that you are part of something larger than yourself can be incredibly empowering.

Consider the benefits of being part of a support group. These groups bring together individuals facing similar challenges, creating a space for sharing experiences, advice, and encouragement. For example, a support group for single mothers can offer practical parenting tips, emotional support, and a sense of camaraderie. Members of the group can share resources, offer babysitting help, or simply provide a listening ear.

Building a strong network requires effort and intentionality. Reach out to people, even when it feels uncomfortable. Foster relationships by being a good friend—listen actively, show empathy, and offer help when needed. These actions build trust and deepen connections, making your support network even stronger.

Community involvement also enhances your resilience by exposing you to diverse perspectives and experiences. Learning from others who have overcome different types of adversity can provide new strategies and insights for dealing with your own challenges. This exchange of knowledge and experience enriches your own coping mechanisms and broadens your understanding of resilience.

Moreover, community support is reciprocal. By helping others, you reinforce your own resilience. Acts of kindness and support create positive energy, boosting your mood and sense of well-being. When you contribute to the well-being of others, you also build your own sense of purpose and self-worth.

In times of crisis, your community can provide critical support. Whether it's offering a meal during a tough time, helping with childcare, or simply being there to talk, these acts of kindness reinforce your ability to cope. Knowing that you have a network of people who care about you can provide immense comfort and strength.

EMBRACE YOUR INNER STRENGTH

Cultivating inner strength, resilience, and confidence is a journey that requires determination, self-love, and support from others. Embrace the challenges that come your way as opportunities for growth. Stay focused on your goals, maintain a positive outlook, and seek support when needed.

With faith, determination, and a supportive community, you can overcome any obstacle and achieve your goals. Remember, you are stronger than you think. Your resilience and inner strength will carry you through even the toughest times.

Embrace your journey, celebrate your progress,
and continue to strive for greatness.

> **"**
>
> *You're beautiful, just the way you are. Shine on. And dare anyone to turn off the lights.*
>
> - Mandy Hale
>
> **"**

Spreading Beauty Through Kindness

I'm excited that you've made it thus far with me. Spreading beauty through kindness is a topic that's close to my heart. There's something incredibly fulfilling about doing kind acts that brighten someone's day or inspire them. So, let's dive into the various aspects of how we can spread beauty through kindness.

THE BEAUTY OF KINDNESS

Acts of kindness can significantly impact both the giver and the receiver, enhancing inner and outer beauty. You might ask yourself, "What can I do to be kind to someone, and how can that help them feel beautiful?" There are countless ways to make a difference.

If you offer a service or run a business, consider donating your services occasionally. For example, if you're a hairstylist, you could volunteer to do hair at a fashion show or offer free haircuts to the homeless. Pull someone aside on the street, offer to cut their hair, give them some clothes, or even a meal. Simple gestures like offering a bagel can brighten someone's day and make them feel valued.

Supporting local businesses is another way to spread kindness. A simple share on social media can significantly impact a small business. You never know who might see that share, and it could lead to significant opportunities for the business owner.

WALKING FOR A CAUSE

Participating in charity walks or runs is another way to show kindness and support. Whether it's a walk for cancer survivors or any other cause that resonates with you, your participation shows empathy, compassion, and support. Wearing a specific color, like pink for breast cancer awareness, and walking alongside others demonstrates solidarity and care, which people deeply appreciate.

Consider organizing a walk or run in your community if one doesn't already exist. You can gather friends, family, and neighbors to join you in raising awareness and funds for a cause close to your heart. These events not only provide physical exercise but also foster a sense of community and shared purpose. Plus, they can be a lot of fun, with participants often dressing up in themed outfits or creating team names and banners.

DONATING CLOTHES

Instead of throwing away clothes during your spring cleaning, consider donating them. Pack them up and take them to the Goodwill or Salvation Army. If you prefer, you can announce it on social media. You never know who might need what you're giving away. For instance, I once had a lot of baby clothes my son had outgrown. I reached out to a friend on Facebook who needed them, and it made her day. Small acts of kindness can leave a lasting impact.

You can also organize a clothing drive in your community. Encourage friends, family, and neighbors to donate gently used clothing and then distribute it to those in need. Partnering with local shelters or community centers can ensure that the clothing goes to those who need it most. This not only helps individuals in need but also fosters a sense of togetherness and collective action in your community.

VOLUNTEERING

Volunteering your time can be incredibly rewarding. I used to volunteer for the Make-A-Wish Foundation, where I helped at local events. You can find numerous opportunities to volunteer in your community by simply searching online. Habitat for Humanity is another excellent option where you can help build homes for those in need. Volunteering not only helps others but also brings a deep sense of fulfillment and purpose.

Think about causes that are important to you and find related volunteer opportunities. Whether it's working at a food bank, tutoring children, or helping at an animal shelter, there are countless ways to give back. Volunteering allows you to use your skills and passions to make a positive impact. It also provides a chance to meet new people and learn more about the challenges and needs within your community.

LOVING YOUR NEIGHBOR

The Bible teaches us to love our neighbors as ourselves. This means being kind, offering your time, and helping out in your community. It doesn't have to be a grand gesture. Simple acts like giving someone your time, effort, or a small act of kindness can significantly impact their life.

Consider starting a neighborhood group where members can share resources, offer help, and organize events. This can create a supportive network where everyone looks out for one another. Small actions, like helping a neighbor with groceries or mowing an elderly neighbor's lawn, can foster a sense of community and make your neighborhood a more welcoming place.

PAYING IT FORWARD

Inspiring readers to spread beauty by uplifting others and making a positive impact in the community is a central theme of this chapter. When you help others, greatness comes back to you. By giving back and looking out for others, you create a ripple effect of kindness. Be the person someone is praying for. Your acts of kindness can turn someone's difficult day around and provide hope and encouragement.

One way to pay it forward is by performing random acts of kindness. These can be small, spontaneous gestures, like buying a coffee for the person behind you in line, leaving a kind note on someone's car, or donating books to a local library. These unexpected acts can brighten someone's day and inspire them to do the same for others.

JOINING CLUBS AND GROUPS

Joining clubs or groups can also make a big difference. For instance, I joined a book club and met new friends who supported my work. Whether it's a book club, a single moms' group, or becoming a mentor for organizations like Big Brother Big Sister or the Boys and Girls Club, there are many ways to get involved and make a positive impact.

These groups provide a platform for sharing experiences, offering support, and learning from others. They also create opportunities for collaborative projects and initiatives that can benefit the broader community. For example, a book club might organize a literacy campaign or a single moms' group might coordinate childcare swaps or job training sessions.

COMMUNITY INVOLVEMENT

If you're part of a local church, reach out to see what events or volunteer opportunities they have. Churches often have various community outreach programs where you can make a difference. Getting involved in community activities not only helps others but also enriches your own life.

Community involvement can take many forms, from participating in clean-up efforts to hosting community dinners or educational workshops. These activities bring people together, strengthen community bonds, and create a sense of shared responsibility and pride.

MENTAL HEALTH AND WELL-BEING

For those looking to improve their mental health or simply need an outlet, consider joining a Zumba class, a dance class, or any activity that brings joy and positivity to your life. Trying something new, like a biking class, can also be incredibly beneficial. Life is too short, and it's never too late to make a positive change in your life and the lives of others.

Physical activities not only improve your physical health but also boost your mental well-being. They provide an opportunity to release stress, improve mood, and connect with others who share similar interests. Look for local fitness classes, sports teams, or outdoor activity groups to join.

A HEART OF KINDNESS

Spreading beauty through kindness starts with self-love and a genuine desire to make a difference. If you have a kind heart and a willingness to help, you can achieve great things. It all begins with the intention to help and the courage to take action.

By engaging in these acts of kindness, you'll not only enhance your own life but also contribute to a more beautiful, compassionate world. So, embrace the power of kindness and let it guide your actions every day. Your efforts, no matter how small, can create significant positive changes in the lives of those around you.

CREATING A KINDNESS CHALLENGE

One way to promote kindness is by creating a kindness challenge within your community or online. Challenge participants to perform a specific number of kind acts within a set time frame, such as a month. These acts can range from simple gestures like smiling at strangers to more involved efforts like organizing a food drive.

Encourage participants to share their experiences and the impact of their actions on social media or through a community bulletin board.

This not only spreads positivity but also inspires others to join the challenge and continue the cycle of kindness.

TEACHING KINDNESS TO CHILDREN

Instilling the value of kindness in children is crucial for fostering a compassionate future generation. Teach your children about the importance of kindness through stories, activities, and by setting a good example. Encourage them to perform kind acts, such as helping a classmate, sharing their toys, or writing thank-you notes.

Involving children in volunteer activities, like serving meals at a soup kitchen or participating in a community clean-up, helps them understand the importance of giving back. These experiences teach empathy, responsibility, and the joy of helping others.

ACTS OF KINDNESS IN THE WORKPLACE

The workplace is another environment where kindness can have a profound impact. Foster a culture of kindness at work by recognizing and appreciating your colleagues, offering help when needed, and promoting a supportive and inclusive atmosphere. Simple acts like bringing in coffee for your team, acknowledging someone's hard work, or offering to assist with a challenging project can boost morale and strengthen team bonds.

Consider organizing team-building activities focused on giving back, such as volunteering together for a local charity or organizing a fundraiser. These activities not only benefit the community but also create a sense of unity and purpose within your team.

SHARING YOUR KINDNESS STORY

Sharing your own acts of kindness and the positive outcomes they create can inspire others to do the same. Use social media, blogs, or community newsletters to share stories of how kindness has made a difference in your life or the lives of others. Highlight the small, everyday acts as well as larger, more impactful efforts to show that every act of kindness counts.

By sharing your story, you not only celebrate the power of kindness but also encourage a culture of generosity and compassion. Your experiences can motivate others to take action and contribute to a ripple effect of positivity.

THE LASTING IMPACT OF KINDNESS

The effects of kindness extend far beyond the initial act. Kindness creates a sense of connection and community, fosters trust and cooperation, and promotes a more inclusive and empathetic society. When we prioritize kindness in our daily lives, we build a foundation for a better world.

Remember that kindness is not just about grand gestures; it's about the small, everyday actions that show we care. Whether it's a smile, a helping hand, or a kind word, these actions add up to create a more compassionate and beautiful world.

ENCOURAGING OTHERS TO SPREAD KINDNESS

Encouraging others to spread kindness can amplify its impact. Lead by example and invite others to join you in your efforts. Whether it's organizing a community event, starting a volunteer group, or simply sharing ideas for kind acts, you can inspire others to make kindness a priority.

Use your voice and platform to advocate for kindness and highlight its importance. Share stories, resources, and opportunities to get involved. By promoting kindness, you contribute to a culture that values compassion, generosity, and connection.

EMBRACE THE POWER OF KINDNESS

Cultivating a habit of kindness enriches your life and the lives of those around you. It fosters inner and outer beauty, creates connections, and makes the world a better place.

By making kindness a daily practice, you can inspire others, build stronger communities, and create lasting positive change. Remember, every act of kindness, no matter how small, has the power to make a difference.

Embrace the power of kindness and let it guide your actions each day. Together, we can create a world filled with beauty, compassion, and love.

> **"**
>
> *Happiness and confidence*
> *are the prettiest things*
> *you can wear.*
>
> *- Taylor Swift*
>
> **"**

Embrace Your Journey

Welcome to the final chapter of this book. If you've made it this far, thank you for reading and accompanying me on this journey. Throughout this book, we've explored many aspects of inner beauty, resilience, and kindness. I hope the stories and insights shared have touched you and inspired growth. This chapter is dedicated to celebrating your journey and encouraging you to continue pursuing self-discovery and empowerment.

REFLECTING ON YOUR JOURNEY

As women, we wear many hats and play numerous roles in our lives. We take care of our families, support our friends, and strive to excel in our careers. Amidst all these responsibilities, it's crucial to focus on our inner selves and nurture our inner beauty. Think back to your childhood. Remember the joy and vibrancy you felt as a young girl. Reconnect with that part of yourself. Reflect on what made you happy as a child and try to incorporate those activities into your life today.

Sometimes, we lose ourselves in the hustle and bustle of daily life. We get caught up in our responsibilities and forget to take care of our own needs. It's essential to take a break, breathe, and reconnect with the things that bring us joy. Whether it's spending a day at the beach, taking a leisurely drive, or simply taking time off to relax, make time for yourself. Embrace self-care and allow yourself to recharge.

EMBRACING INNER BEAUTY

Inner beauty is about loving yourself and finding joy in the little things. It's about surrounding yourself with positive influences and being mindful of your surroundings. Everything in your life—your friends, your job, the music you listen to—affects your inner self. Focus on cultivating a positive environment that supports your growth and happiness.

Ask yourself what brings you joy. What motivates you to get up in the morning? Are you starting your day with positive affirmations and setting a positive tone for the day? Practice self-love and do things that make you happy. Be free, be fun, and don't let worries consume you. Take breaks when needed and prioritize your well-being.

SPREADING POSITIVITY

Spreading positivity to others can be as simple as giving someone a compliment or a smile. If you see someone having a tough day, take a moment to uplift them. Small acts of kindness can have a significant impact on someone's day.

Acts of kindness, no matter how small, can make a big difference. Hold the door open for someone, offer a genuine compliment, or simply smile at a stranger. These small gestures can brighten someone's day and create a ripple effect of positivity. When you make a conscious effort to spread kindness, you contribute to a more compassionate and connected world.

THE POWER OF KINDNESS

Kindness is a powerful tool that can transform lives. Proverbs 11:25 says, "A generous person will prosper; whoever refreshes others will be refreshed." This scripture highlights the importance of giving and the rewards that come with it. When you give kindness and love to others, you receive goodness in return.

Consider the ways you can incorporate kindness into your daily routine. Volunteer at a local charity, donate to a cause you care about, or simply offer your time to someone in need. Kindness doesn't have to be a grand gesture; even the smallest acts can have a profound impact. When you make kindness a habit, you not only improve the lives of those around you but also enrich your own life.

EMPOWERMENT THROUGH SELF-DISCOVERY

Empowerment begins with self-discovery. Continue to explore and learn about yourself. Study your behaviors, reactions, and triggers. Understand what brings you joy and what causes you stress. By understanding yourself better, you can navigate life's challenges more effectively and make choices that support your well-being.

Every day is an opportunity to grow and learn. Embrace the journey of self-discovery and don't be afraid to make mistakes. Learn from them and use them as stepping stones to become a better version of yourself. No one is perfect, and everyone has their own journey. Celebrate your progress and keep moving forward.

BUILDING A SUPPORTIVE COMMUNITY

Surround yourself with positive influences and supportive people. Whether it's friends, family, or a community group, having a support system is essential. Engage in activities that bring people together and create a sense of community. Volunteer, join clubs, or participate in local events. Building strong connections with others enhances your own well-being and creates a network of support.

A supportive community provides a safety net during challenging times. When you have people who care about you and want to see you succeed, you're more likely to stay motivated and overcome obstacles. Cultivate relationships with people who inspire you, challenge you, and support your growth.

PERSONAL GROWTH AND DEVELOPMENT

Personal growth is a continuous process. Just as we invest time in our careers and education, we should invest in our personal development. Read books, attend workshops, and seek out mentors who can guide you. Learning from others and gaining new perspectives can significantly enhance your personal growth.

Identify areas of your life where you'd like to grow and set goals for yourself. Whether it's improving a skill, developing a new habit, or expanding your knowledge, continuous learning and self-improvement are key to personal growth. Celebrate your progress and stay committed to your journey of self-development.

RESILIENCE AND DETERMINATION

Resilience is the ability to bounce back from setbacks and keep moving forward. Life will inevitably throw challenges your way, but it's how you respond that matters. Adopt a mindset of determination and tunnel vision. Focus on your goals and keep pushing forward, even when things get tough. Remember that every setback is an opportunity for growth and learning.

Life's challenges can be daunting, but they also provide opportunities to build strength and resilience. When faced with adversity, remind yourself of your past successes and the obstacles you've already overcome. Use these experiences as a source of strength and motivation. Believe in your ability to navigate through difficult times and emerge stronger on the other side.

GIVING BACK

Giving back to your community and helping others can bring immense joy and fulfillment. Whether it's volunteering your time, donating to a cause, or simply being there for someone in need, acts of kindness have a powerful impact.

They not only help others but also enrich your own life. Consider how you can make a difference in your community. Look for opportunities to volunteer, support local initiatives, or mentor someone in need.

Giving back not only helps those around you but also fosters a sense of purpose and connection. It reminds us that we are part of a larger community and that our actions can contribute to the greater good.

ENCOURAGING OTHERS

Encouraging others and being a positive role model can inspire those around you. Share your journey and experiences, and let others see the strength and resilience you possess. Your story can motivate and uplift others, showing them that they too can overcome challenges and achieve their goals.

Be open about your struggles and triumphs. Sharing your experiences can create a sense of solidarity and provide valuable lessons for others. Encourage those around you to pursue their dreams, face their fears, and believe in themselves. Your words and actions can have a profound impact on someone else's life.

CELEBRATING YOUR ACHIEVEMENTS

Take time to celebrate your achievements, no matter how small they may seem. Recognize your progress and give yourself credit for your hard work. Celebrating your successes boosts your confidence and motivates you to keep striving for more.

Create traditions to mark your achievements. Whether it's treating yourself to something special, sharing your success with loved ones, or simply taking a moment to reflect and appreciate your progress, celebrating your achievements reinforces your commitment to your goals and encourages continued growth.

EMBRACING YOUR TRUE SELF

Embracing your true self is a crucial part of this journey. It means accepting yourself, flaws and all, and understanding that your worth is not determined by external validation. It's about finding confidence in who you are and letting your authentic self shine through.

Self-acceptance is a powerful tool for building inner strength and resilience. When you accept yourself, you free yourself from the pressures of trying to conform to others' expectations. You allow yourself to grow and evolve in a way that is true to your values and beliefs. Embrace your uniqueness and celebrate what makes you different.

OVERCOMING SELF-DOUBT

Overcoming self-doubt is a vital part of the empowerment journey. Self-doubt can be a significant barrier to achieving your goals and realizing your full potential. It's important to recognize when self-doubt is holding you back and take steps to overcome it.

Challenge negative thoughts and replace them with positive affirmations. Surround yourself with supportive people who believe in you and encourage your growth. Take small steps towards your goals to build confidence and demonstrate to yourself that you are capable and strong.

THE ROLE OF GRATITUDE

Gratitude plays a significant role in fostering a positive mindset and enhancing overall well-being. Take time each day to reflect on the things you are grateful for. This practice can shift your focus from what's lacking to what's abundant in your life.

Keep a gratitude journal where you write down three things you're thankful for each day. This simple practice can help you cultivate a more positive outlook and increase your resilience. Gratitude reminds us to appreciate the present moment and recognize the blessings in our lives.

DEVELOPING A GROWTH MINDSET

Developing a growth mindset is essential for personal and professional development. A growth mindset is the belief that abilities and intelligence can be developed through dedication and hard work. This mindset encourages a love for learning and resilience in the face of challenges.

Embrace challenges as opportunities for growth. View failures as learning experiences rather than setbacks. Stay curious and open to new experiences. By adopting a growth mindset, you empower yourself to continuously improve and achieve your goals.

FINDING BALANCE IN LIFE

Finding balance in life is crucial for maintaining your well-being and happiness. It's easy to become overwhelmed by the demands of work, family, and personal responsibilities. Strive to create a balanced lifestyle that allows you to take care of your physical, emotional, and mental health.

Set boundaries to protect your time and energy. Make self-care a priority and ensure you have time for relaxation and activities that bring you joy. Balance work with leisure and make time for the people and activities that matter most to you.

CONNECTING WITH OTHERS

Building meaningful connections with others is a vital part of personal growth and empowerment. Surround yourself with people who inspire you, support your goals, and challenge you to be your best self. Seek out mentors, join groups that align with your interests, and be open to forming new relationships.

Engage in activities that allow you to connect with like-minded individuals. Whether it's joining a book club, participating in community events, or attending workshops, these interactions can provide valuable support and inspiration. Building a strong network of supportive relationships enhances your resilience and provides a sense of belonging.

EMBRACING CHANGE

Embracing change is essential for personal growth and development. Change can be challenging, but it also presents opportunities for growth and new experiences. Approach change with an open mind and a positive attitude.

Adaptability is a key skill that helps you navigate life's transitions. Embrace new opportunities, learn from your experiences, and remain flexible in the face of uncertainty. By embracing change, you allow yourself to grow and evolve, leading to a more fulfilling and enriched life.

PRACTICING MINDFULNESS

Practicing mindfulness can significantly enhance your well-being and personal growth. Mindfulness involves being present in the moment and fully engaged with your surroundings. It helps reduce stress, improve focus, and enhance emotional regulation.

Incorporate mindfulness practices into your daily routine. This can include meditation, deep breathing exercises, or simply taking a few moments each day to pause and reflect. Mindfulness helps you stay grounded and connected to your inner self, fostering a sense of peace and clarity.

SETTING INTENTIONS

Setting intentions is a powerful practice that guides your actions and decisions. Intentions are different from goals; they focus on the present moment and your desired state of being. Setting intentions helps you align your actions with your values and create a sense of purpose.

Each morning, take a few moments to set your intentions for the day. Reflect on how you want to feel and what you want to focus on. This practice helps you stay centered and mindful throughout the day, ensuring your actions are purposeful and aligned with your goals.

CELEBRATING DIVERSITY

Celebrating diversity is an important aspect of creating a compassionate and inclusive world. Embrace the differences in others and appreciate the unique perspectives they bring. Diversity enriches our lives and broadens our understanding of the world.

Encourage inclusivity in your community and celebrate the diverse backgrounds and experiences of those around you. This fosters a sense of belonging and mutual respect, creating a more connected and empathetic society.

THE IMPORTANCE OF REST

Rest is essential for maintaining your physical, emotional, and mental well-being. In our fast-paced world, it's easy to overlook the importance of rest and relaxation. Make time for rest and ensure you get enough sleep each night.

Incorporate relaxation techniques into your daily routine. This can include activities like reading, taking a warm bath, or practicing yoga. Rest allows your body and mind to recharge, ensuring you have the energy and focus needed to pursue your goals.

THE JOURNEY AHEAD

As you move forward, remember that your journey is unique and personal. Embrace the challenges and celebrate the victories. Stay committed to your personal growth and continue to seek out opportunities for learning and development. Each day presents a new opportunity to grow and evolve. Embrace the journey with an open heart and a curious mind, trusting that you have the strength and resilience to navigate whatever comes your way.

Self-empowerment is an ongoing process filled with ups and downs. Each experience, whether a success or a setback, contributes to your growth and development. Reflect on the lessons you've learned throughout this book and apply them to your daily life. Share these insights with others, inspiring and uplifting those around you. Your journey is unique, and your impact on the world is significant.

Keep shining, keep growing, and continue to embrace your inner beauty and strength. You have the power to create a beautiful and meaningful life. Your story, your actions, and your kindness have the potential to make a profound impact on the world.

> **"**
>
> *When you're a beautiful person on the inside, nothing in the world can change that about you. Jealousy is the result of one's lack of self-confidence, self-worth, and self-acceptance. The Lesson: If you can't accept yourself, then certainly no one else will.*
>
> *- Sasha Azevedo*
>
> **"**

Author's Note

Thank you for being a part of this journey. I hope the stories and insights shared have inspired you to embrace your inner beauty, spread kindness, and pursue self-discovery. Remember that you are not alone, and we are all in this together. Continue to empower yourself and uplift others. Your journey, with its challenges and triumphs, is yours to shape with love and determination.

Stay connected with me and join my community. Follow my journey, and let's continue to inspire and uplift each other. Together, we can create a world filled with beauty, kindness, and compassion. Your journey of self-empowerment is a testament to the strength and resilience within you.

Email: booksbytejumade@gmail.com
Website: www.touchedbytejumade.com

Acknowledgments

The completion of this book marks a significant milestone, made possible only through the support, love, and encouragement of many impactful individuals. As I look back on this journey, my heart is filled with gratitude for those who have stood by me, inspired me, and lifted me along the way.

To my mom (Mary Lee), my best friend (Evette Tucker), and my family:

Thank you for always standing by my side! From sharing laughter to shedding tears and praying like warriors, your positivity and inspiration mean the world to me. I truly appreciate you! Life has its ups and downs, highs and lows, and it's crucial to remember that the lows are temporary. Having the support of loved ones is invaluable, no matter the size of your circle, because true love never fails. I appreciate all you have done.

To every photographer, designer, model, hairstylist, makeup artist, and fashion team I've ever worked with:

You rock! Each of you has inspired me in some way, shape, or form. Thank you for your relentless creativity and hard work. May everything you do continue to prosper.

About the Author

Tejumade Ogunmokun has always been a hardworking individual with a strong passion for creativity. From a very young age, she knew she was gifted with many talents, such as writing, drawing, and engaging in various creative pursuits. Whether styling hair, personal styling, or walking with natural grace and confidence, Tejumade has consistently exhibited poise and eloquence. These attributes eventually led her to participate in major fashion shows such as NY Fashion Week, WALK, and many more up and down the East Coast, all while creating a powerful name for herself in the industry.

Tejumade has also been featured in many magazines and graced the cover of Cie Fashion Magazine in 2017, published by Damian Saunders. She is well-versed in the fashion industry and has written columns offering Model 101 advice for COPA Style Magazine, published by Rodney Branch. Her extensive experience in the fashion world has opened many great opportunities, allowing her to see all facets of the industry. She enjoys serving as a guide to upcoming models and artists, encouraging them to acknowledge not only their exterior beauty but also to admire their inner selves.

In this book, Tejumade shares many motivating stories of self-love, overcoming insecurities, serving the community, and more. Tejumade is a strong, passionate, funny, motivating, and extremely driven individual. Once she sets her mind on doing something, she does it with all her heart and soul, putting forth her best efforts. She is a true business-woman with a diverse background.

In early 2021, she launched a beauty cosmetic line known as *Touched by Tejumade*, which focuses on women's empowerment. This is where you can see Tejumade come to life—from modeling to skincare to serving and uplifting others, she is dedicated to fulfilling her purpose.

The birth of her amazing son, who is the joy of her life, inspired her to pivot from her modeling career and focus on being the best role model for him and herself. It was then that she delved deeper into her inner self to become a positive figure for him. This is when her true love for writing blossomed into a children's book based on journaling.

She has written scriptures, songs, and letters to her son, and to this day, she has grown to be a best-selling author. Her goal with "Beneath the Surface" is to inspire and create a lasting impression within her community. This book is not only for aspiring models but also for young African American women and adults. It serves as a guide to accept every flaw you may have by learning to love yourself while maintaining a lasting relationship with God.

To get in touch with Tejumade Ogunmokun, please contact her here:
Email: booksbytejumade@gmail.com